PIANO • VOCAL • GUITAR

Hannah Montana

SONGS FROM AND INSPIRED BY THE HIT TV SERIES

ISBN-13: 978-1-4234-2475-8
ISBN-10: 1-4234-2475-1

WALT DISNEY MUSIC COMPANY

DISTRIBUTED BY

HAL•LEONARD®
CORPORATION

7777 W. BLUEMOUND RD. P.O. BOX 13819 MILWAUKEE, WI 53213

In Australia Contact:
Hal Leonard Australia Pty. Ltd.
4 Lentara Court
Cheltenham, Victoria, 3192 Australia
Email: ausadmin@halleonard.com

Visit Hal Leonard Online at
www.halleonard.com

THE BEST OF BOTH WORLDS

Words and Music by MATTHEW GERRARD
and ROBBIE NEVIL

*Recorded a half step higher.

WHO SAID

Words and Music by MATTHEW GERRARD,
ROBBIE NEVIL and JAY LANDERS

'Cause some can talk the talk, ___ but this girl just wants to rock. ___

___ I'm in - di - vid - u - al; ___

___ I'm not like an - y - one. I can be glam -

- or - ous, ___ just like you see in all the mag - a - zines. ___

hold - ing back. Stay - in' right on track, 'cause you con -

trol the game, __ so let 'em know your name. No

lim - i - ta - tions on i - mag - i - na - tion. I - mag - ine __ that! __

Guitar solo ad lib.

JUST LIKE YOU

Words and Music by ANDREW DODD
and ADAM WATTS

So what you see is on - ly
be treat - ed

half the sto - ry; there's an - oth - er side ___ of me.
dif - f'rent - ly. ___ I wan - na keep it all ___ in - side. ___

I'm the girl you know, but I'm
Half the girl time I've got ___ my

PUMPIN' UP THE PARTY

Words and Music by
JAMIE HOUSTON

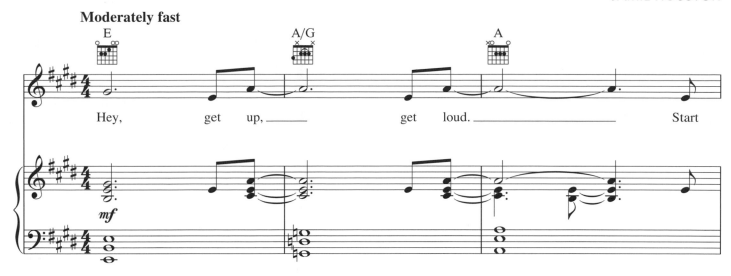

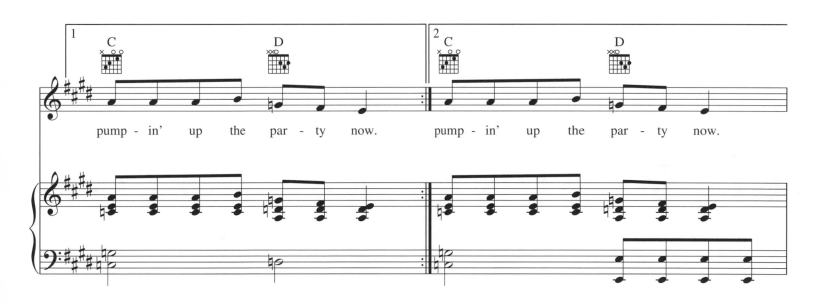

IF WE WERE A MOVIE

Words and Music by JEANNIE LURIE
and HOLLY MATHIS

I GOT NERVE

Words and Music by JEANNIE LURIE,
KEN HAUPTMAN and ARUNA ABRAMS

THE OTHER SIDE OF ME

Words and Music by MATTHEW GERRARD,
ROBBIE NEVIL and JAY LANDERS

Recorded a half step higher.

THIS IS THE LIFE

Words and Music by JEANNIE LURIE
and SHARI SHORT

hold on ___ tight. ___

And this is a dream. _____ It's

all I ___ need. _____ You

nev - er know where you'll find it, _____ and

POP PRINCESS

Words and Music by
BEN ROMANS

SHE'S NO YOU

Words and Music by MATTHEW GERRARD,
JESSE McCARTNEY and ROBBIE NEVIL

They got a lot-ta girls who know they got it go-in' on,   but noth-ing's ev - er a com par - i - son to you.
They got a lot-ta girls who dance in all the vid-e-os,   but I pre-fer the way you do, the way you move.

Now, can't you see that you're the on - ly one I real-ly want   and ev-'ry-thing I need is ev-'ry-thing you do?
You're more than beau-ti - ful and I just wan-na let you know   that all I ev - er need is what I got with you.

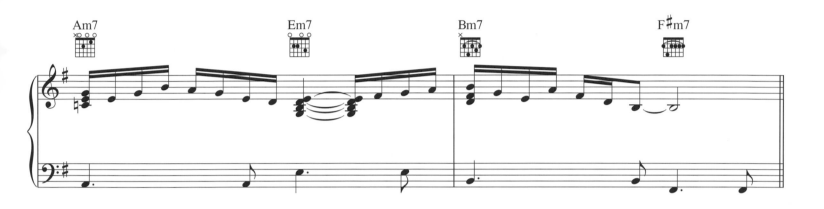

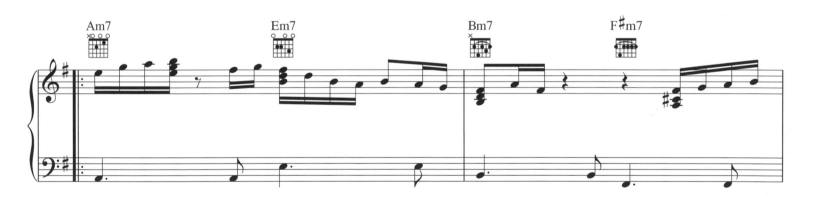

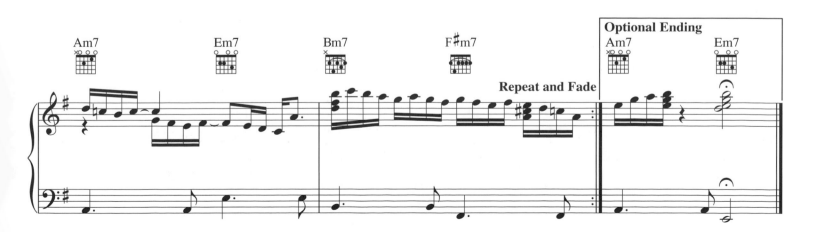

FIND YOURSELF IN YOU

Words and Music by MATTHEW GERRARD, AMBER HEZLEP,
JULIA ROSS and SARAH ROSS

SHINING STAR

Words and Music by MAURICE WHITE,
PHILIP BAILEY and LARRY DUNN

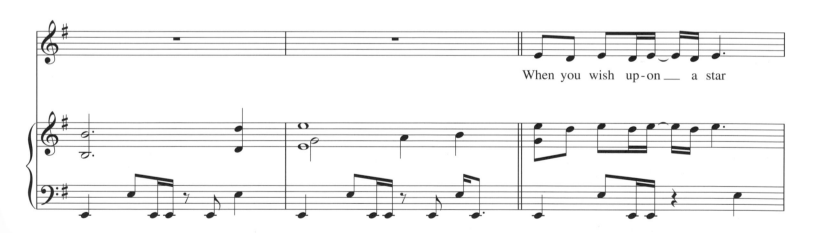

When you wish up-on __ a star

(when you wish up-on __ a star), your dreams will take you ver - y far, yeah, __

yeah, __ yeah, yeah. __ When you wish up - on __ a dream

(when you wish up - on __ a dream), life __ ain't al - ways what __ it seems. __

Once __ you see __ your light __ so clear, __

in __ the sky, __ so ver - y dear. __

Shin-ing star __ come in - to view, shine __

__ its watch - ful light __ on you, _____ yeah. ___

Gives you strength __ to car - ry on and make my bod - y big and strong. ___

I LEARNED FROM YOU

Words and Music by MATTHEW GERRARD
and STEVE DIAMOND

Lyrics:
I did-n't wan-na lis-ten to what you were say-ing. I thought that I ___ knew all I need to know. ___

ques - tion. That's a les - son that I learned from

you. _____

We al - ways don't a - gree on what is the best ___